BETTER THAN OUR BEST: WOMEN OF VALOR IN AMERICAN HISTORY

By

Arlene Ferman
Helene Svihra
Grace A. Aqualina

ILLUSTRATED BY:
Grace A. Aqualina

BRANDEN
Publishing Company, Inc.
Boston, MA

Library of Congress Cataloging in Publication Data
Ferman, Arlene, 1939-
  Better than our best : women of valor in American
history / by Arlene Ferman, Helene Svihra, Grace
A. Aqualina.
        p. cm.
  Includes bibliographical references.
  Summary: Presents biographical sketches of nine
distinguished American women, including Mary Ludwig Hays
McCauley (Molly Pitcher), Harriet Stratemeyer Adams, and
Beatrice Alice Hicks.
  ISBN 0-8283-1941-3 : $9.95
  1. Women--United States--Biography--Juvenile
literature. 2. Women--United States--History--Juvenile
literature. [1. United States--Biography.]
I. Svihra, Helene, 1920- . II. Aqualina, Grace A.,
1942- . III. Title.
  HQ1412.F47 1990
  920.72--dc20   90-32866
                                             CIP
                                              AC

BRANDEN
Publishing Company Inc.
17 Station Street
Box 843 Brookline Village
Boston, MA 02147

ACKNOWLEDGEMENTS

The authors wish to acknowledge The Women's Project of New Jersey, Inc. for use of materials and information from their collection of biographies.

TABLE OF CONTENTS

Come back with us in time and see
What we have done in history.
Follow our footsteps down the street;
Within this book our paths will meet.

Listen to what our voices say
To all of you in school today.
Learn what obstacles we met,
And how we overcame them. Yet,
Although we had a price to pay,
We kept our course. It was our way.

When you have traced our lives within
This book, have faith; you, too, can win.
Whatever in life you may endeavor,
Keep courage in your hearts forever!

Mary Ludwig Hays McCauley--Molly Pitcher

MOLLY PITCHER BEING PRESENTED TO
GENERAL WASHINGTON

This oil painting is signed by Dennis Carter, 1856. It shows Molly
Pitcher meeting George Washington on the field of battle at
Monmouth. Courtesy of the Collections of Monmouth County
Historical Association, Freehold, New Jersey.

Mary Ludwig Hays McCauley--Molly Pitcher

Mary Ludwig Hays McCauley, whose nickname was *Molly Pitcher*, became famous as the American Revolutionary War hero in the Battle of Monmouth.

1

Mary Ludwig was the daughter of German immigrants who came to America in 1730. It is believed that she was born on October 13, 1754, on her family's dairy farm near Trenton, New Jersey.

2

As a young girl, Mary helped with the chores on her family's farm. She was strong, muscular, and very talkative.

3

At 15, Mary's parents arranged for her to work as a domestic in the home of Dr. William Irvine in Carlisle, Pennsylvania. Although her name was Mary, she was given the nickname *Molly*.

4

While working in Carlisle, Molly met the village barber, John Casper Hays, whom she married on July 24, 1769. She took his name and became known as Molly Hays.

5

When John Hays first enlisted in the army in 1775, Molly went back to work for Dr. Irvine. However, Molly joined her husband when he later transferred to a Pennsylvania regiment stationed near Trenton.

6

At that time, many wives followed the troops to do the laundry, nursing, and most of the cooking. This work was needed because the army did not provide these important services for the soldiers. The women worked in exchange for food.

7

JUNE 28, 1778

The Battle of Monmouth was fought on June 28, 1778, when the colonists caught up with the British near Freehold, New Jersey. When the battle began, Molly stayed and worked. It was a hot, steamy day. Many soldiers were failing from the heat.

8

While Molly suffered under these same battlefield conditions,
she helped the soldiers stay strong by carrying water to them from a nearby well.
When the soldiers saw her they would call, "Here comes Molly with the pitcher." Many even called her "Captain Molly."

9

On one trip Molly reached her husband's cannon just as he was wounded. With no one left to man the cannon, Molly took up the rammer staff and loaded and fired the cannon. Molly kept firing the cannon while General George Washington's troops fought the British to a standstill.

10

Private Joseph Plumb Martin, a witness to Molly's actions on the battlefield, gave this account:
"While in the act of reaching a cartridge and having one of her feet as far before the other as she could step, a cannon shot from the enemy passed directly between her legs without doing any other damage than carrying away the lowest part of her petticoat."

11

After the battle Molly and her husband returned to Carlisle where John Hays recovered from his wounds.
Some time later, Molly gave birth to a son, John Ludwig Hays.

12

Molly's husband died two years after they settled in Carlisle. In 1792, Molly married John McCauley and became known as Molly McCauley. Because John McCauley could not support the family, Molly went to work doing laundry and taking care of the children of other families.

13

Thirty years later, when Molly was 68 years old, the Legislature of the state of Pennsylvania granted her $80 a year for her services during the Revolutionary War.

14

At her death on January 22, 1832, she was buried in the Old Graveyard in Carlisle, Pennsylvania. In 1876, local citizens of Carlisle put up a gravestone in her memory. The date was July 4, 1876, the 100 year anniversary of the adoption of the Declaration of Independence.

15

In 1978, a 10-cent postcard was issued in Molly's honor by Congress and the United States Postal Service.

16

11--Better Than Our Best

BRAVERY is courage, valor,
fearlessness in face of danger,
heroism.

Molly Pitcher
distinguished herself
at the Battle of
Monmouth. She was a
hero.
But Bravery is not only
in battle. It can be
seen in everyday life.
We act bravely when we do
something that we were at
first afraid to do.

Example: Amy was afraid to
stand in front of her class
to give a book report. She
had to build up the courage
to be able to do it. However,
once she did, she felt good
about herself.

Molly Pitcher with Cannon--
Courtesy of Special Collection
and Archives Rutgers University Libraries.

ACTIVITIES

1. Imagine that you are living in the time of Molly Pitcher. You are living on a small farm close to the Battle of Monmouth. You can hear the firing of the cannons. After the battle you hear about a woman named "Molly" who showed bravery on the battlefield. Write a letter to a friend describing what you understand Molly Pitcher did at the Battle of Monmouth.

2. Look at a commemorative postage stamp. Then look at the picture of Molly Pitcher on page 5 at the beginning of this chapter. Design your own commemorative postage stamp featuring Molly Pitcher.

QUESTIONS AND ACTIVITIES

1. Describe Molly Pitcher's bravery on the battle-field.

2. Suppose that you were Molly Pitcher. Would you go to battle as she did?

3. How did Molly's childhood prepare her for the work she did on the battlefield?

4. When Molly Pitcher fired the cannon at the enemy during the Battle of Monmouth she wore a long skirt like other women of her time. However, over the skirt she wore a soldier's coat and hat. Why do you suppose Molly put on a soldier's coat and hat?

5. During the Revolutionary War, there were women who courageously worked beside their husbands on the battlefield as Molly Pitcher did. The following is a story taken from *Stories of New Jersey* by Frank R. Stockton, Rutgers University Press, New Brunswick, N.J., 1961 of another woman who acted bravely in the Revolutionary War. Her name was Mrs. Jinnie Waglum.

15--Better Than Our Best

One day Mrs. Waglum went to visit a friend near her home in Trenton, New Jersey. While there she learned that General George Washington was planning to march his troops from Trenton to Princeton, New Jersey. Washington did not want to use main highways for travel for fear the enemy might see him. But Washington could not find anyone who knew the area well enough to guide the troops to Princeton. When he learned of Mrs. Waglum's offer to help him take his troops over back roads to Princeton, he was willing to have her guide them. He knew that would be the safest way to travel. So Jinnie Waglum put on a soldier's coat and a soldier's hat, much like Molly Pitcher did, mounted a horse and headed General Washington's troops. She led the men on roads she often traveled going through Quaker Bridge to Princeton in time for the battle.

In what way did each woman, Molly Pitcher and Jinnie Waglum, show great courage? Was there a time in your life that you acted courageously? Tell about it.

6. Molly Pitcher went back to private life after the war. It was said that she was always kind and helpful to her neighbors and friends. Describe someone in your neighborhood or community or family who is like Molly Pitcher in kindness and caring of other people.

CLASSROOM DISCUSSIONS AND ACTIVITIES

1. Life has changed from the time Molly Pitcher lived to today. What is the difference in our homes, our way of travel, our clothing, our cooking style?

2. Why did America fight the Revolutionary War? Who were the British? What led to the Battle of Monmouth? Discuss why women at times followed their husbands to battle. How might the war be different had women not been there? What might their lives have been like if they hadn't gone? What happened to the children during the fighting?

3. It is believed that Mary McCauley's (Molly Pitcher) parents came from Germany. Locate Germany on a map of Europe. How do you suppose immigrating to a new country was for Mary's parents? What hardships might they have had? What new and pleasant things might they have found? Tell how you would feel leaving your home to travel to an unknown place to live.

Using a world map, trace the route your great grandparents, grandparents, parents, or other relative used to come to America. Use a different color crayon for each person.

17--Better Than Our Best

Cornelia Hancock

Reproduced from *A Brief History of Laing School...1866-1926* courtesy of the Friends Historical Library, Swarthmore College

Cornelia Hancock

Dear Cornelia Hancock

Dear Emily

***

Letters from a young girl to
Cornelia Hancock, nurse, teacher,
social reformer.

Replies from Cornelia Hancock on
her life's experiences.

The following text portrays the story of Cornelia
Hancock's life taken from Cornelia's own letters. In
the text, letters are written by a fictitious pen pal,
Emily. Cornelia Hancock's answers are based upon
her published letters in which she described the events
of her life from 1863 - 1865. We have rewritten them
as if she were writing them today.

July 15, 1863

Dear Miss Hancock,

I heard that you are a volunteer nurse in the army. One of the wounded soldiers returning home to Philadelphia told stories of how you helped the wounded at Gettysburg, Pennsylvania. He said that you are a Quaker. I thought that Quakers are brought up not to participate in war.

I also heard that the women who go to war to be nurses have to be accepted by Dorothea Dix who is head of the Female Nurse Corps. Miss Dix wants all nurses to be middle-aged and married. It is said that you are young and pretty. Why did you want to go to war?

I hope you have time to write to me.

Your admirer,
Emily

July 25, 1863

Dear Emily,

How nice of you to write to me. I am 23 years old and a nurse in the army. Ever since President Lincoln recognized a state of civil war on April 15, 1861, I knew that I would someday want to serve my country.

I would visit my sister, Ellen, and her husband, Dr. Henry Child, in Philadelphia, and hear talk in their home about slavery and how groups were formed to aid runaway slaves. Before too long, I asked my brother-in-law to help me become a nurse. I was told that I would not be accepted for nursing duty because I was too young. I wanted to serve my country. And it is not easy to stop me when I want to do something.

I left for the war on July 5, 1863, when Dr. Child sent his carriage to fetch me. After arriving in Philadelphia, Dr. Child and I boarded a train with a nurses' delegation led by a Miss Eliza Farnham. We were headed for Baltimore and then on to Gettysburg. In Baltimore, I met Miss Dix who promptly told me that I was too young to go to war. While Miss Farnham and Miss Dix were arguing about this, I decided to just go aboard the train anyway. When we arrived at Gettysburg there was such a great need to help the wounded that there was no further argument about age.

Your friend,
Cornelia Hancock

August 6, 1863

Dear Miss Hancock,

I received your letter. Thank you for writing. With the war the way it is, my family cannot get supplies for our farm. Every now and then we see a soldier returning home wounded from the war.

You must have been scared to see so many sick and dying men at Gettysburg. I don't think I could have been there. I heard that there was so much fighting and so many wounded. How did you help them?

I like writing to you. I hope we can be pen pals.

Your admirer,
Emily

August 15, 1863

Dear Emily,

Our train arrived at Gettysburg on the evening of July 6. The shooting was over. I walked into a church which was being used as a hospital for the wounded. Inside were hundreds of desperately wounded men stretched out on straw-covered boards placed across the high-back pews. The faces of these men were white with pain. I was face to face with them.

I set to work doing what I could. I had no formal training and no supplies, but I did have paper, pencil, and stamps. So I went from soldier to soldier that night writing letters for them to their families and friends. This was hard to do. To listen to these very sick and wounded men tell me what to write home brought tears to my eyes.

The following morning I went to visit a field hospital five miles from Gettysburg. There I saw the real horrors of war. Many men lay dying. Others were severely wounded. Not knowing what to do, I quickly looked for something for them to eat. Wagons of bread and supplies were arriving, and I took some food. I sat down in a patch of grass with a loaf of bread in one hand and a jar of jelly in the other. Near me were a dozen wounded men watching--tired, hungry, and needing care. Having no spoon, fork, or knife, I spread the jelly over small portions of bread with a stick and fed the wounded. I had the joy of seeing them appreciate the little bit of food I could find. Helping the soldiers was the reason I came to war.

23--Better Than Our Best

As each hour passed we saw more and more doctors, nurses, hospital supplies, and food arrive. Each day was better and better for the hurt and disabled. But that first day, the sixth of July, three days after the battle, was a time that one could not even imagine possible.

I enjoy reading your letters. Yes, I would like to be your pen pal. If I can, I will answer your questions.

Your pen pal,
Cornelia Hancock

Cornelia Hancock at Gettysburg

August 22, 1863

Dear Miss Hancock,

You must be very busy helping all the wounded soldiers. My brother went off to war. I was sad to see him go.

What did your parents think about you going off to war?

Wishing to know,
Emily

25--Better Than Our Best

August 31, 1863

Dear Emily,

I was very sad to be leaving my parents as your brother must have been sad to leave home. Until I left for Gettysburg, I had been living at home at Hancock's Bridge, New Jersey, where I was born on February 8, 1840. Hancock's Bridge was settled by my ancestors, so the village took my family's name. It is one of the most historic towns in America. I am very proud to be part of New Jersey's history in this way. My parents, Rachel and Thomas Hancock, raised five children in the house we inherited from my grandparents. My mother always thought that I should do what I felt I would like to do. Probably that is why there was little said when I went off to Gettysburg. Mother is a Quaker woman, always dressed in Quaker style, with a full-skirted dress that is to the floor and a white apron over the dress. Often, she wears a shawl across her shoulders.

Father attends no church. He believes that everyone should believe in himself or herself.

Your friend,
Cornelia Hancock

September 26, 1863

Dear Miss Hancock,

My brother wrote to us this week. I thought of you and how you helped the wounded at Gettysburg write letters home. My brother told me that the soldiers in Gettysburg hospitals had a medal made for you as a way of saying thank you for helping them. You are their hero. You saved many of their lives. My brother said that you have blonde hair, blue eyes, and stand only five feet tall. That is just how I pictured you.

I am very proud to know you, even though it is only through our letters. I wish I could meet you.

Your admirer,
Emily

November 24, 1863

Dear Emily,

In September, I returned to Philadelphia with Dr. Child and then visited Hancock's Bridge. I did not stay long. There was still work to do to help the war effort. In October, I left for Washington, D.C. to help with the freed slaves.

The medal you mentioned in your last letter was presented to me by the soldiers at Gettysburg. On one side it reads: "Miss Cornelia Hancock presented by the wounded soldiers 3rd Division 2nd Army Corp." The other side reads: "Testimonial of regard for ministrations of mercy to the wounded soldiers at Gettysburg, Pa. July - 1863." This medal will be my dearest possession, and I will keep it all my life.

Your friend,
Cornelia Hancock

December 23, 1863

Dear Miss Hancock,

    It is almost Christmas and the war is still on. It will not be the same for us as it was years ago when the family was all together for the holidays. I think of you and what you are doing to help so many people. By the time this reaches you, it will be a new year.

    Please write and tell me what you are doing now.

                                Your pen pal,
                                Emily

February 21, 1864

Dear Emily,

For the past two months, I have taken charge of the Washington Contraband Hospital where all the sick and wounded black soldiers, all sick servants serving officers in the army, and the sick in general around Washington come for care.

In early February, Secretary of War Edwin Stanton gave me a pass to visit anywhere in the lines of the Union Army. Soon after, I was asked to work at the Second Corps Hospital at Brandy Station, Virginia. This was much more to my liking than Washington, so I left for Brandy Station on February 11th.

When I arrived, one hundred and fifty men had just been brought in from the battlefield. Things are different here than at Gettysburg. There is not as much chaos.

There are eight huge hospital tents that are clean and neat and have lots of supplies. There are also separate tents for eating and a separate cookhouse. Conditions have improved for the soldiers since the beginning of the war.

Your friend,
Cornelia Hancock

May 2, 1864

Dear Miss Hancock,

I heard that General Ulysses S. Grant issued orders for all civilians to go home.   I do not know where to write to you, so I am sending this letter to Hancock's Bridge.

Please answer me soon,
Emily

31--Better Than Our Best

June 30, 1864

Dear Emily,

Your letter reached me at Hancock's Bridge. It has been a long time since I wrote to you. I went with Dr. Child, as his assistant, aboard the steamer, Wawasset, bound for Belle Plain, Virginia. When we arrived on May 12th, I could not believe my eyes. At the wharf, there were 3000 wounded men -- hungry, exhausted, hardly able to move. I was the first nurse to arrive. We worked all night feeding the wounded and putting them on board the steamer for hospitals in Washington.

I went on to Fredericksburg, Virginia, to help after the Battle of the Wilderness. Here supplies were limited and there was no end to the wounded. However, the suffering did not seem as great as at Gettysburg because the wounded were in houses.

On May 28th, we left Fredericksburg for White House Landing, Virginia. We traveled many days by wagon train under almost constant enemy gunfire, cannons, and snipers. There were 8000 soldiers in the wagon train. All showed much bravery. At night we slept in our clothes, sometimes in the wagons, other times in an abandoned shanty. When we passed a stream, we splashed cold water on our hands and face. I cooked and made coffee for the men and cared for the hurt and wounded. I was thankful I got through the march safely.

We were told we had to leave White House Landing quickly when the rebels opened a volley of fire. Again we traveled in a long wagon train. It was during this ride that a gun shell hit the rear of our wagon. No one was injured, and we continued on to City Point, Virginia, where we are now.

Your friend,
Cornelia Hancock

33--Better Than Our Best

August 20, 1864

Dear Miss Hancock,

I know you have been working very hard. There have been stories about you in the newspapers. It said that you were the first lady to arrive at Fredericksburg to aid and care for the wounded. It told all about you helping the sick and wounded, feeding them, caring for them, and never tiring.

It was wonderful to read about you. People call you "the Florence Nightingale of America."

I'm glad I know you.

Always your pen pal,
Emily

The following text is presented as excerpts from Emily's diary as she might have recorded the events in Cornelia Hancock's life after the Civil War.

EMILY'S DIARY

NOVEMBER 14, 1865
After the war, Cornelia Hancock was invited to attend the Grand Military Review in Washington, D.C. She sat in the President's Grandstand. What an honor that must have been.

APRIL 22, 1866
Cornelia Hancock wrote to tell me how happy she was to be working in Mt. Pleasant, South Carolina. She was teaching the freed slave children in a war-torn church, using charcoal to write on the white walls. Soon she would have pencils, paper, and books for the children provided by the Philadelphia Friends Association for the Aid and Elevation of the Freedman. She was proud of the work she was doing.

DECEMBER 20, 1870
It is almost Christmas. This is the time of year that I think of Cornelia the most. We have written to each other for seven years now. She is still in Mt. Pleasant and still enjoying her work at the school.

35--Better Than Our Best

OCTOBER 22, 1875

Cornelia returned home from the South. It is now 10 years since she started her school for the freed slave children. The school was named the Laing School after Mr. Henry Laing who donated most of the needed supplies. Blacks in the South revered Cornelia and told their children about her and her good work. She helped them learn to read and write. She got them clothes to wear and seeds to plant so that they would not have to wear rags and not have to go hungry.

Cornelia was not feeling well when she returned to her sister's house in Philadelphia. After a short rest, she went off to England to study social work.

NOVEMBER 12, 1878

Today I met Cornelia Hancock for the first time. It has been more than 15 years since I first wrote to her. We have become good pen pals. It was wonderful to finally meet her. She is still pretty with her hair still blonde and her eyes so blue. She really does stand just five feet tall.

JANUARY 14, 1892
There have been articles in the newspapers about Cornelia. After returning from England, she and a friend, Edith Wright, have been in the Wrightsville section of Philadelphia helping the poor improve their living conditions through better schools, sanitation, and recreation. Cornelia has been working hard. She helped establish the Society for Organizing Charity and the Children's Aid of Pennsylvania. She was on the committee that hired the first paid social worker for the Society, and she was the secretary of the Society's first Board of Directors.

DECEMBER 31, 1927
Cornelia Hancock died today at the home of her niece in Atlantic City, New Jersey. She was 87 years old.
I will sadly miss her.

QUESTIONS AND ACTIVITIES

1. News of what Cornelia Hancock did during her time as a volunteer nurse in the army was reported in several newspaper articles. Write an article about Cornelia Hancock and what she did to help in the war effort. Describe her. How did she help the wounded? What did she do to help the children of the slaves? How did Cornelia Hancock contribute to society?

2. At the end of the chapter on Cornelia Hancock, Emily continues by sharing her diary. Keep a diary for two weeks, longer, if you like.

3. Make a time line of special events in your life. Use the time line given in this chapter as an example.

4. Write an essay on how you would like to be known as a person contributing something to society.

CLASSROOM DISCUSSIONS AND ACTIVITIES

1. What is a volunteer? Have the class discuss and list volunteer jobs. Have a discussion on ways the students would like to volunteer their time in school - in their community.

2. The Battle of Gettysburg was fought near Gettysburg, Pennsylvania. Discuss living conditions of the townspeople at that time, including life style, clothing, where the battle was in relation to the town, where the wounded were cared for, and how Cornelia Hancock must have felt as she cared for the wounded.

3. Talk about pen pals. Discuss what can be learned by having a pen pal. Arrange to have the students choose a pen pal and have an ongoing class project with pen pals.

TIME LINE

EVENTS IN THE LIFE OF CORNELIA HANCOCK

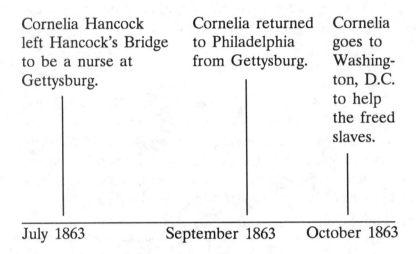

Cornelia Hancock left Hancock's Bridge to be a nurse at Gettysburg.

Cornelia returned to Philadelphia from Gettysburg.

Cornelia goes to Washington, D.C. to help the freed slaves.

July 1863   September 1863   October 1863

The above is a time line giving events in Cornelia Hancock's life.

Events can span months or years.

Using this as an example, make up a time line of events in your life.

Lydia Young Hays With Bull

Lydia
Young Hays

"A Woman of Vision"

Perhaps it was the smell of flowers. Perhaps the fresh summer breeze blowing across the meadow reminded me of that fateful day so many years ago. I remember how blue the sky was. The great field I was crossing was a waving carpet of green and yellow grasses dotted with fists of color from all the wildflowers. If only I hadn't stopped to pick some of those flowers. If only I had taken the regular route home instead of the shortcut to the farmhouse. Perhaps today I would be sighted and not completely blind. Can I ever forget the terrible sound of the bull rushing wildly toward me? The memory of that enormous animal mowing me down and knocking me out will never leave me. I hate what the bull has done to me, robbing me of my sight. Yet, because of this terrible accident, I was able to help so many blind people in this country.

I was born Lydia Young Hayes on September 11, 1871. It is now 1942, and I am back in Minnesota on my nephew's farm in Bemidji. As I sit here on the porch, all the smells of late summer flood my mind with memories. I am so proud of what I was able to do. If my parents had not sent me to my uncle's home in Massachusetts, I never would have been educated at the Perkins Institution. This school was also known as The Massachusetts School for the Blind. I stayed there until I graduated from high school. My parents were wise to send me! They wanted to be sure that I would learn to grow and think and do.

I did well. I continued to study at the Boston Kindergarten Normal School, a school to train teachers of young children. I was given the opportunity to manage a private nursery for sighted children. Although I enjoyed working with children, I knew I had to do something with my education to help other blind people. I volunteered to be a home teacher and then to do private tutoring. This last job took me to Ohio. Finally, when Massachusetts allowed blind people to be taught at home, I was asked to return there and implement this program with another teacher. That was in 1900. I stayed for eight years.

In 1909, I was selected to organize the New Jersey Commission for the Blind. After only one year, Governor Woodrow Wilson appointed me, Lydia Hayes, to be the Commission's first chief executive officer. I was stunned. To appoint a woman to any executive position was unusual, but to appoint a blind woman was incredible. My heart burst with pride.

I knew I had tremendous work to do. I established the Commission's first headquarters in downtown

43--Better Than Our Best

Newark. We were so lucky! A friend provided us with a ten room house at 14 James Street. This wonderful friend accepted no rent at all. We were able to provide social rooms, classrooms, workshops, and offices. The caretakers were a blind couple. At least, blind people had a place to go for help when they wanted it.

The New Jersey Commission for the Blind also served blind people in another way. A registry of every blind person living in New Jersey was formed. After one year, there were 750 people registered.

Although we were able to do many things, the work became harder and harder. We knew we had to make sure the rights of the blind were protected. All policies and practices had to insure those rights within the state. After all, people without sight could work, go to school, and serve others as others served them. One is not helpless if one is blind! It had always disturbed me that many sighted people felt the blind should be in their own special schools. Why? I could not understand why a blind child should not function in a regular school. So I fought and fought hard so that these children could receive an education in a normal public school! We won. New Jersey allowed public schools to conduct classes using Braille. The state even gave financial help for these classes. It was also important that the prevention of blindness be stressed. In 1910, another teacher and I set up such a class in the Newark Public Schools. I am proud to say that these classes were used as models for other school systems across the country.

I knew this would do wonders for blind people and sighted people alike. After all, each individual must learn about his or her responsibility to the community. And, of course, the community must recognize and promote the capabilities of every individual.

Five years later, in 1915, industrial jobs were open to the blind. This was a great opportunity for blind people to enter the regular working world. People would be able to see just how capable blind people were. The Commission began a Home Teaching Service Program to teach Braille, typing, and how to produce handicrafts that could be sold. We even implemented a Home Industries Program to market anything made by blind people.

Now, here is my birthday once again. I am 71 years old. As I sit on the porch of my nephew's farmhouse with all those memories, I can't help thinking about that terrible accident with the bull. Yet, I was able to accomplish so much even though I was blind.

QUESTIONS AND ACTIVITIES

1. What do you admire most about Lydia Hayes?

2. Many blind people use guide dogs. Find out how guide dogs are trained.

3. What have you done in your life that makes you proud?

4. Read *Follows My Leader* by James Garfield. With your parents' permission, try to eat blindfolded using the method given in the book.

CLASS DISCUSSIONS AND ACTIVITIES

1. Learn the Braille code. Write secret messages to your friends in Braille.

2. List famous people who are handicapped and their accomplishments. For example, Stevie Wonder is one such person. Do you know any handicapped people in your family or neighborhood? With your parents permission speak to them and discover their accomplishments.

3. Write sentences using descriptive expressions like "waving carpet of green and yellow grasses" and "fists of color."

4. People of all ages accomplish many different things. Some of the accomplishments are very big (i.e. discovering a vaccine for a particular disease), and some accomplishments are small, personal triumphs (i.e. learning the twelve times table). What things have you accomplished so far that give you a source of pride? What things would you like to accomplish in your lifetime? Make a bulletin board display showing what the class has accomplished and your hopes for the future.

Lydia Hayes as Teacher

ELIZABETH COLEMAN WHITE

BIOGRAPHY

Born on October 5, 1871, on her parents' cranberry farm in New Lisbon, New Jersey, Elizabeth Coleman White grew up to become a self-taught scientist. Her parents, Mary Fenwick and Joseph J. White had four daughters. Elizabeth was the oldest.

EARLY YEARS
As a young girl, Elizabeth often went with her father on his weekend visits to her family's cranberry farm. In 1887, after graduating from the Friends Central School in Philadelphia, Elizabeth began working on the farm. She worked in the bogs where she helped supervise cranberry pickers during the harvest season. In the winter months she took courses in first aid, photography, dressmaking, and millinery at Drexel University in Pennsylvania.

AND THEN...

As time went on, Elizabeth became more interested in the farm's operation and more involved in the packing and shipping of cranberries to all parts of the country. Her great love was Whitesbog, the name given to the farm, and she enjoyed being part of her family's business.

AS A PEACEMAKER

Elizabeth knew many of the cranberry pickers and their families personally. Some were from the Pinelands, an area of New Jersey that is mostly marshlands suitable for growing cranberries and blueberries. Other pickers were from Philadelphia. Over the years, Elizabeth watched many of their children grow up. In 1910, when the National Child Labor Committee reported poor treatment of children helping to pick cranberries, Elizabeth felt the charges were wrong. She wrote letters and spoke often in behalf of the children and their families, stating that the seven weeks of harvest time trained them to be self-supporting. For four years, Elizabeth and the National Child Labor Committee continued this controversy until the National Labor Committee printed a retraction in the *Trenton Times*, and Elizabeth was acknowledged as a peacemaker.

ACCOMPLISHMENTS

In 1911, Elizabeth read a United States Department of Agriculture report on Frederick Coville's work in blueberry propagation. Because Elizabeth had always wanted to raise blueberries to sell at the markets, she wrote to Coville inviting him to continue his research at

Whitesbog, now the farm she worked with her father. Coville accepted the offer. For the next five years, Elizabeth White and Frederick Coville worked together. White located wild blueberry bushes by asking local Pineland people to help her find the best blueberries from the wild bushes. She wrote out directions for them to follow and named a bush after its finder. She was known as "Miss Lizzie" to the area woodsmen who taught her all about berry size, flavor, and ripening. She offered from one to three dollars to the woodsmen for marking the largest berry on any bush. Thousands of cuttings were taken to create the new varieties. In 1916, White and Coville produced the first commercial crop of blueberries.

Elizabeth White was the first to use a cellophane wrapper, a clear plastic covering that was put over the small baskets of blueberries when they were shipped to stores for sale. In 1927, Elizabeth helped organize the New Jersey Blueberry Cooperative Association. In 1986, New Jersey's blueberry industry was second in the country in total production of blueberries.

LATER LIFE

In her later life, Elizabeth's interest included all plants of the Pine Barrens. Her home at Whitesbog, called Suningive, had all varieties of these plants in her garden. She formed her own business, Holly Haven, Inc. and sold many varieties of holly plants, as well as other plants of the Pine Barrens. She wrote about her life's work and gave talks to horticultural clubs and radio audiences.

Elizabeth Coleman White died at the age of 83 on November 11, 1954, at Whitesbog.

AWARDS
Elizabeth White was the first woman member of the American Cranberry Association. She was the first woman to receive the New Jersey Department of Agriculture citation, and she received the highest medal from the Horticultural Societies of Massachusetts and Pennsylvania.

Elizabeth Coleman White, 1928

Courtesy of New Jersey Conservation Foundation.

HISTORY OF WHITESBOG DATES BACK TO 1857

Whitesbog is part village and part farm owned by the state of New Jersey since 1966. It was, at one time, a self-contained company town that even had its own post office, store, and water supply. Eighty men worked full time on the farm, and 600 migrant workers came in to harvest the crops of cranberries and blueberries during the harvest season. Whitesbog was started by Elizabeth White's grandfather, Colonel James A. Fenwick, a pioneer cranberry farmer who started farming in 1857. Fenwick had 108 acres that later became a 3,000 acre plantation managed by Elizabeth's father, Joseph White.

Today, Whitesbog remains much as it was in the early 1900's. Although some of the buildings are long since gone, most of the original village is intact. Whitesbog is located in Lebanon State Forest, near Browns Mills, New Jersey.

Wheater Update

Today's forecast calls for sunny skies, hot, with a high of 92° F low of 82° F.

Blueberry Facts

** Blueberries are round, plump and purplish-blue in color

** Blueberries grow only in acid soil. To insure cross pollination, two varieties must be planted next to each other.

** The United States and Canada grow more blueberries that are sent to market than the rest of the world combined.

** Explorers to our continent noted that the American Indians harvested the wild crops of berries, used them in their cooking, besides eating them raw.

(See FACTS page 2)

FACTS
(continued from page 1)

The early pioneer families learned from the Indians how to substitute the berries for a sweetener. They also made jellies and jams from the berries.

POETRY CORNER

BLUEBERRIES

"You ought to have seen what I saw on my way
To the village, through Patterson's pasture today:
Blueberries as big as the end of your thumb,
Real sky-blue, and heavy, and ready to drum
In the cavernous pail of the first one to come!
And all ripe together, not some of them green
and some of them ripe! You ought to have seen!"

(excerpt from "Blueberries" from *The Poetry of Robert Frost* edited by Edward Connery Lathem, Holt, Rinehart & Winston, N.Y. 1969)

INQUIRING REPORTER

WHAT IS YOUR FAVORITE WAY OF EATING BLUEBERRIES?

LISA	LENNY	HEATHER	MARC
"With whipped cream"	"Just plain"	"In my cereal"	"In pancakes"

Ask Jeffrey
What are cranberries?

Cranberries are fruits that are tart and red in color. They grow as a trailing, slender shrub in fields known as *bogs*. Cranberries need an acid soil and damp ground to grow. Cranberry sauce and cranberry bread are two ways of eating and enjoying cranberries.

BLUEBERRY RECIPES
Grandma Jenny's Quick and Easy Blueberry Desserts

** Crush blueberries, add sugar and serve over vanilla ice cream.

** Top pound cake with blueberries and whipped cream

DID YOU KNOW THAT...?

* Elizabeth White had a dream of planting fields of blueberries. As a young girl growing up on her family's cranberry farm she would hunt the largest and best flavored blueberries that grew wild around the cranberry bogs while she thought of starting blueberry fields from cuttings.

* Elizabeth's idea for cultivating the blueberry probably came from her grandfather, James Fenwick, who was one of the first to cultivate the cranberry in the mid 1800's.

* Blueberry growers around the world are indebted to Elizabeth Coleman White for developing the first cultivated blueberry.
Today blueberry farming is a large business.

* The first quarts of blueberries shipped to market by White in 1916 were covered with brown paper fastened with tape. A few years later, after seeing cellophane wrappers on candy boxes, White started to use cellophane. Blueberries were one of the first fruits to be marketed with a cellophane wrapping. The clear wrap makes it easy to see the fruit and protects the blueberries.

* The Pine Barrens of New Jersey is where the cranberry and blueberry grow wild. Today, as we eat blueberries, we remember that it was Elizabeth White who worked almost her whole life, taking the blueberry from its wild state of growing to its development as a cultivated fruit sold in markets. She worked with Frederick Coville from the United States Department of Agriculture to create 68,000 different blueberry plants in her lifetime.

QUESTIONS AND ACTIVITIES

1. Why were Elizabeth White's job, hopes, and dreams important to us?

2. What do you most admire about Elizabeth White?

3. Have you ever thought of doing something that was never done before? Would you like to try? Write about it.

4. Elizabeth White enjoyed going to Whitesbog when she was young. Write about what you enjoy doing with a parent, grandparent, or relative. Perhaps you took a trip or worked in your family store or visited with a family member at work.

5. What ways do you imagine you are like Elizabeth White? What ways are you different?

6. Design a poster or leaflet that you would use to encourage people to collect samples of blueberries. (See the poster used by Elizabeth White in 1914 as an example.)

7. Collect favorite family blueberry or cranberry recipes. Or make a recipe file of blueberry or cranberry recipes you might enjoy eating. Publish some of your recipes in a class newspaper. Try some recipes in a cooking class.

Poster used by Elizabeth White in 1914.

CLASSROOM DISCUSSIONS AND ACTIVITIES

1. What helped Elizabeth White become a leader in her field? Discuss leaders you know such as a teacher, principal, political leader, librarian, clergy. What does that person do? How does she or he affect other people and contribute to society?

2. Elizabeth White was a woman who worked in her family business. Tell about women you know who work in a business. What do they do in that business? What position do they hold in the business? Is it a family owned business?

3. Plan to do a class newspaper. Divide the class into departments: editor, managing editor, news editor, news writers, art editor, artists, sports editor, sports writers, feature editor, feature writers, food editor, circulation director, advertising department, special projects. Visit a newspaper. Discuss ways to make your newspaper fit the needs of the class and how many issues you plan to publish. Pick a name for the paper.

ALICE PAUL

"Alice Speaks"

<u>Characters</u>

Alice Paul
Tacie Paul - her mother
William Paul - her father
Young Woman - a college friend
Narrator
Three Quaker women
Two groups of people - three men and a woman; two
women and two men

Time: Winter - 1973
Place: A cottage in Ridgefield, Connecticut
Setting: Alice Paul is seated in a high-back chair near
the fireplace. A telephone is at her side. It rings; she
picks it up.

ALICE: Yes, yes, this is Alice. No, you're not bothering me. Having a nap? Me? Heavens no! No time for that. Do you think I'm an old lady just because I'm 87. I've been waiting for your call. What is the latest report on the vote? *(She listens.)* We must have a stronger, more organized campaign. Our key people in every state must work harder if we want the states to ratify this amendment. *(She listens to the caller.)* Let me know how the campaign in Indiana is going. I want to be informed of all developments. Goodbye.

[She replaces the receiver and leans back in the chair. She smooths her hair and laughs.]
Why am I laughing? These young women who have taken on this battle must think I'm all washed up. It seems I've spent my whole life - first in my mind, and later in actions - campaigning to light the fires for the rights of women, and I haven't lost a spark of hope yet.

[She leans forward and gazes into the fireplace.]
Just like those flames, my desire for freedom for women still burns brightly. Of course, what they do with this freedom is up to them. It is our business to see that they are free.
[She settles back in her chair. Still gazing at the fire, she speaks.]
What would Mother and Father have thought of how far we've come? I can still see them in the parlor of our home in Moorestown, New Jersey. Moorestown - the farms, Main Street with its small shops and tall trees. No telephones, then.
[Lights fade on her. She sits back and closes her eyes. On side-stage, her mother and father appear - in her imagination. Tacie Parry Paul, her mother and William

61--Better Than Our Best

Mickle Paul, Jr., her father. They are seated in their parlor dressed in the period of the late 1890s.]

TACIE: What a serious girl our Alice is, William. Always reading, reading. They say at the Friends School she's their best student. And the librarian tells me she just reads books on Quakers and reformers. She's wearing out Charles Dickens'books here at home. His books are filled with stories of injustice. Do you ever wonder what mark she'll make in the world with her head filled with all that knowledge of the wrongs people have suffered?

WILLIAM: How could she miss her mark in life? She's the dependable one, you know. You can always count on her if there's a job to be done.

TACIE: You know, William, I feel sometimes that Alice has the spirit of her grandmother, Alice Stokes, inside of her. Alice Stokes was a true Quaker, opposing slavery, working for the community, and education. Why there might never have been a Swarthmore College without her help.

WILLIAM: Our Alice's future is in her own hands and mind, Tacie. Quaker women, like Quaker men, have always been free to speak and to work for freedom and quality for all races and people. But always peacefully - never with violence.
   [Lights fade on them. Alice walks to the window. She gazes at the falling snow.]

ALICE: Mother and Father are always in my thoughts. Their examples of caring about others taught me so much. I remember going with Mother to a meeting in Moorestown in 1900. It was then that I learned about how hard women were working for the right to vote. It took another 20 years of campaigning and hard work to finally win that right. Now we're still working to win rights for women under the Constitution. We're still at it.

[She walks to the telephone near the window and dials. Lights fade on her. Side stage: A young woman appears dressed in the fashion of the early 1900s.]

YOUNG WOMAN: How well I remember Alice Paul. When she arrived at Swarthmore College she was only 16. What fun she was! The pranks she played on everyone! They were harmless, of course. Then Alice became serious. She began to study hard and read late at night. Professor Brooks had a major influence on her. When he spoke about going out and making the world a better place, she told us her life would be dedicated to this cause.

[Alice is still standing before the window, no longer on the telephone.]

ALICE: In the summer of 1905, I left my Quaker world of college and Moorestown and went to New York City. I went to a new world of immigrant families, and my first project was helping to organize a milliner's union to protect the rights of men and women who were working in the hat-making trade. But I knew I needed more challenges, and I got those in England. I'll never forget the meetings of the suffragists there. I was still young enough to be shocked when people jeered and shouted down the speakers at the votes for women meetings. I joined the group called the Women's Social and Political Union. I know now this was the beginning of my life's work. My path was before me.

[Alice sits and folds her hands as if she were in school long ago.]

NARRATOR: Yes, and that path brought her to exciting and painful times. After joining the Women's Social and Political Union, Alice was arrested in England and Scotland in 1909. How many prison terms did Alice serve? Three. Just for making speeches about votes for women or shouting "Votes for Women" at public meetings. And then came the hunger strikes. "No vote, no food!" they said. Well, Alice was there with her English friends, joining in the hunger strike. How could anyone imagine that the authorities would force feeding tubes down their throats so that the hunger strike wouldn't make them martyrs? When she was released, Alice threw a feeding tube at the Lord Mayor of London while he was making a speech.

[Alice walks to the fireplace to stir the logs.]

ALICE: *(laughing)* My path was not the Quaker way. We are supposed to be non-violent. I thought I could never go home again.

[She returns to the chair beside the fire and taps the telephone. Lights fade and three women with placards appear.]

FIRST WOMAN: But home she came to Moorestown. Her behavior in England had shocked us all. A Quaker in jail, throwing bricks through windows! Unheard of.

SECOND WOMAN: But Alice spoke to us about the suffrage movement. She wrote articles in newspapers and pamphlets and made so many of us believe as she did.

THIRD WOMAN: We joined her in summer street marches, carrying signs like these.
[She shows the placard, "Votes for Women". Lights fade on women. A spotlight shines on Alice.]

ALICE: The memories of the earlier years of our struggle seem so vivid even now. We began with so little, no funds at first. It was like starting a campfire with a spark from dry twigs. But it grew! I wonder how many remember that first big parade in Washington, D.C., in 1913. We marched five thousand strong that day. President Woodrow Wilson, who had just been elected, was wondering where all the people were who should be standing along the route he was taking to the White House. Where were they? Watching us. It did become ugly when some of the spectators pushed us and jeered at us. Some tore the banners from our hands. But it became front page news. And through the power of politics, we women waged war against President Wilson and Congress to approve the Nineteenth Amendment which would give women their right to vote. In 1920, the long parade had reached its rest after 72 years of marching. Yes, it was in 1848 when the first women's rights convention met in Seneca Falls, New York.

[Alice stands and begins to walk - pacing as if on a picket line.]

I can still hear the voices of the people during our march in front of the White House in 1917.

[Several people appear.]

FIRST MAN: We were young boys when Alice and the suffragists came to Washington. We saw them marching on the sidewalk in front of the White House. Remember, Ted?

SECOND MAN: Yes, I sure do! We watched them as they were put into police vans. They were carried off to jail for "obstructing the sidewalk." I remember my mother and father reading the paper about it and Mama saying, "Why those women are being fed by tubes down their throats because they refuse to eat." Then we heard lots of people say it was a shame. Even those against the vote for women began to sympathize.

WOMAN: My sister, Grace, said that Alice was like Joan of Arc. I was 14 at that time. Even when they put her in the insane ward, nothing could or would change her. She had spirit, courage!

THIRD MAN: She won, she won! When one group is denied a right, we all suffer!

[The lights fade on the men. Alice picks up the telephone. She dials, then puts the receiver down.]

ALICE: Busy. That's good. It means they're working - communicating. Communication. That's the key to understanding and progress. I remember - after we won the vote we knew we had to continue our work for equal rights for women and men. It was back in 1923 when, after writing the ERA, we were able to get it introduced in Congress. What the Equal Rights Amendment means is that both men and women have equal rights under the law. Both are protected equally because it is wrong to keep even one person from getting equal justice. That is why I convinced the United Nations to put the rights of all people, including the women of all nations, into its charter. The dignity and worth of the human person is paramount.

[Alice walks to center stage.]

NARRATOR: In 1972, the Senate passed the ERA with a vote of 84 to 8. It seemed one sided, but much work needed to be done. Thirty-eight states had to agree to it in order for the ERA to become part of the Constitution. Alice Paul knew that the seven years allotted to the passage of this proposed amendment was not enough time.

ALICE: No, seven years are not enough. We need more time. Too many forces are misinterpreting what ERA is all about. It's about equal rights to jobs and pay, and opportunity for all. Thousands of women have worked hard for this for many years - half a century so far.

[The telephone rings. Alice sits in her chair
to answer it. Two men and two women appear.]

67--Better Than Our Best

FIRST WOMAN: Alice Paul was right - seven years were not enough. She died in 1977. Only three more states were needed to pass the ERA. Congress voted to extend the 1979 deadline until 1982. In 1982, the time ran out and the proposed amendment died.

FIRST MAN: Alice Paul was among the first to show how people without power could use non-violent methods to protest a wrong.

SECOND MAN: She led the struggle to add women to the Civil Rights Act of 1964 - no one can be discriminated against in getting a job because of race, religion, or sex. And today, women can expect equal pay for equal work. It wasn't like that before.

SECOND MAN: Alice Paul spent almost her whole life working with and for women all over the world, not only here in the United States. She studied and became a lawyer so that her knowledge of law could help in the fight for women's rights.

FIRST WOMAN: Alice wrote the Equal Rights Amendment and was a leader of this movement for more than 45 years. Although the ERA had failed to become part of the Constitution, many believe that one day it will succeed. Alice Paul will always be remembered for her struggle to achieve the right to vote for half the citizens of the United States and to include equal rights for women in the Constitution.

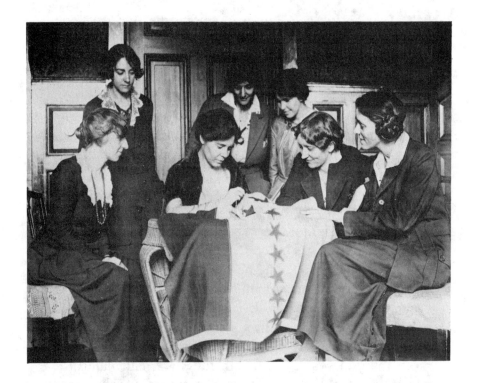

Alice Paul Sewing Ratification Star onto Suffrage Banner 1920 (Courtesy of Schlesinger Library, Radcliffe College).

QUESTIONS AND ACTIVITIES

1. Research other leaders of the women's movement. Write about these other leaders of the women's movement (for example, Susan B. Anthony).

2. Have a roving reporter interview various people in the school giving their opinion about the ERA and women's rights.

3. Make a study of President Woodrow Wilson: his life and accomplishments. How did he help or hurt the campaign for women's right to vote?

4. Do you admire Alice Paul as much as the men and women in the play seem to admire her? Why or why not?

5. How was her life important to men as well as women?

6. Do you think you could endure all the punishment she had to take to pursue her dreams? Do you have something special you would like to do when you are older? Do you think it might require special bravery to achieve this goal? Explain.

7. Have you read about or heard about anyone else who has experienced many obstacles to achieve their goals? Write a story about it.

8. Alice Paul was a Quaker. Find out where the Quakers founded their colonies in America and what their beliefs were.

CLASSROOM DISCUSSIONS AND ACTIVITIES

1. The struggle for women's right to vote began in 1848. Many women and men worked for the struggle for the right to vote here in America. Research who these women were and where they carried on their work. Trace their activities on a mural to show the progress from 1848 to 1920.

2. In the play, some of the characters speak of the Quaker way of non-violence to protest a wrong. Discuss Mahatma Ghandi and Martin Luther King, Jr. and their methods of protest. How were they the same? How were they different?

3. "When one group is denied a right, we all suffer...", this is a line from the play. What does this mean to you? Can you give examples of this? Your examples can come from history or from what is happening in the world today.

4. With permission of your teacher, stage a protest march of your own. Use an issue like that of Alice Paul or other issues that affect us in the world today. Find an example of events in our country or some-where else in the world where people are protesting a wrong. Make a placard and write speeches to support your opinions.

5. If you could change just one thing you believe is wrong today, what would it be? How would you go about changing it? Write about it in either play or story form.

Harriet Stratemeyer Adams
circa 1980

(Photograph courtesy of Simon & Schuster, Inc)

HARRIET STRATEMEYER ADAMS

"Treasures in the Trunk"

The rain pelting against the tall windows in the living room sounded as if someone were throwing fistfuls of sand. I tried to continue reading my book, but it wasn't holding my interest.

Why is it, I wondered, books I read now just don't seem to keep my interest the way the books I read as a child did? Sighing, I let the book drop to the floor. I got up from the sofa.

I wandered around the house for a bit. No one was home. It was very quiet, almost too quiet. I went into the kitchen, searched the refrigerator, and found nothing exciting to eat. I wandered upstairs to my room thinking I really should clean my room. I decided against that and started to go back downstairs when I heard the attic door open. It often did that during a storm. The drafts from the attic always seemed to come through. Instead of slamming it shut, however, I switched on the light and climbed the dusty stairs to find myself standing amid boxes, bags of old clothing, and items my family had collected for years.

"I really should go through this stuff," I murmured. I moved a large plastic bag and discovered my grandmother's old black trunk. I smiled as I remembered how as a child I had been so fascinated with it.

"Please, can't you unlock it so I could see all the treasures?" I used to beg.

"What kind of treasures do you think are in there?" my grandmother would smile as we played our little game.

"Gold coins, diamonds - real big ones, like baseballs, lots of pearls and stuff from pirate ships and ..."

My grandmother would laugh. "It seems everyone likes pirates."

Now, all these years after my grandmother's death, the padlock of the trunk hung open, hooked loosely through the lock. I slipped it off and opened the lid. Its rusted hinges squeaked loudly, but the lid stayed open. Inside was a tray about 3 inches deep divided into two compartments. Each was filled with envelopes, papers, faded ribbons, and old photographs. I lifted the tray out of the trunk and placed it on the floor.

You never know, I thought, there just could be treasures of gold in there.

There weren't. Instead, I saw piles of old books and a folder of old newspaper clippings. I lifted out a dull, green book with faded printing on its spine. As I turned it over, I discovered a picture of two small children dressed in old-fashioned clothes. They were walking along the seashore holding hands. The little girl was holding a doll dressed in a white sailor suit while the boy held a shovel and pail. The title was *Bunny Brown and His Sister Sue* by Laura Lee Hope.

Gingerly, I opened the cover only to discover several pages loose and slipping out of the book. I realized the book was old. It had been published in 1916. No wonder the children were dressed so differently. I couldn't imagine children today dressed like that.

I looked inside the trunk again and realized there were so many old fashioned books. There were four more green ones about Bunny Brown and his sister Sue. Lifting out more piles of books, I noticed there were two more series written by the same author. One, *The Outdoor Girls*, I didn't remember. But I did remember the next set about the Bobbsey Twins. I could remember all those rainy days when I was glued to these books, fascinated by the adventures of the two sets of twins. After all, my brother Andy and I are twins. But these books were not the ones I remembered reading. These books, published before World War I, showed the twins in very old fashioned clothes and hairstyles.

These really are treasures, I thought to myself. They must have belonged to my grandmother when she was a little girl. Imagine, they were treasures to her at one time. Or else she wouldn't have saved them all these years. I found two more series in the trunk. One, the Nancy Drew books, I knew very well. I had prided myself on having read every single adventure of the girl detective. The other, *The Hardy Boys*, was one of Andy's favorites.

I shivered as I felt a draft come through the attic walls. I put most of the books back in the trunk. I was very careful not to drop them, fearing some of them would fall apart. Once I had closed the trunk carefully, I gathered the remaining books and the newspaper clippings and took them downstairs.

Spreading the clippings out on the dining room table, I noticed that the various series of books were written by three different authors. Laura Lee Hope, who wrote about Bunny Brown and his sister Sue, also wrote the Bobbsey Twins and the Outdoor Girls. Carolyn Keene wrote all the books in the Nancy Drew and Dana Girls series. The Hardy Boys was written by Frank L. Dixon.

This is odd, I thought. These books were written by different people, yet they all sound somewhat alike. I wondered.

As I went through the articles, I discovered one with a photograph of a small, gray haired woman. Harriet Stratemeyer Adams was her name. The impish smile on her face made me think she knew a big secret and just recently let people know about it.

She was born on December 11, 1892, in Newark, New Jersey, exactly fifty years before I was born. Her father, Edward, was a famous author who made up stories spontaneously. He entertained Harriet and her little sister Edna with adventures. Edward Stratemeyer began publishing his first series of books, *The Rover Boys*, in 1899. Because he had so many stories to tell, Harriet's father hired several people to write for him. He paid them a salary and developed the Stratemeyer Syndicate. He published over 800 books this way.

While her father was building his Syndicate, Harriet grew up and graduated from Barringer High School in Newark and attended Wellesley College in Massachusetts. In 1914, Harriet Stratemeyer graduated from college and wanted to work at a newspaper. Her father would not give his permission because he did not consider it proper for young women to work for a living. When Harriet insisted, her father hired her to work for him in his Syndicate. Harriet learned many skills such as editing, and she learned her father's formula for his successful series.

After one year, Harriet Stratemeyer married Russell Adams and settled in Maplewood, New Jersey. For the next fifteen years, she did not write or edit for the Syndicate; she worked at home raising her four young children. During this period, she also worked hard in unpaid positions teaching Sunday School and serving the Girl Scouts. She even began a new literary magazine for the Women's Club of Maplewood.

In 1930, Edward Stratemeyer died. Unfortunately, he left no directions for what should happen to his seventeen series of books including *Tom Swift*, *The Bobbsey Twins*, *The Hardy Boys*, and the first three books of *Nancy Drew*.

Harriet and her sister, Edna, inherited the Stratemeyer Syndicate. Rather than disband, the sisters continued what their father had started.

Harriet Stratemeyer Adams used different pseudonyms when she authored the Syndicate's most successful series. These authors' names are still widely known by many children today. The most famous are: Carolyn Keene, Frank L. Dixon, and Laura Lee Hope. She also wrote as Victor Appleton II in Tom Swift, Jr., May Hollis Barton in the Barton Books for Girls, Ann Sheldon in Linda Craig, and Helen Louise Thorndyke in the Honey Bunch books.

Harriet Stratemeyer Adams, like her father, hired many writers to write more adventures for each series. The writers were required to use the Syndicate Formula. It was very easy to follow. The first page had to hook the reader immediately, while the last page of every chapter had to be a cliff-hanger. Each chapter had to be filled with adventure, suspense, intrigue, and humor. There could be no lying, bad language, or violence in any of her books. Harriet Stratemeyer Adams researched many places in many different countries including our own, so that the settings for the books would be authentic. In 1982, Harriet Stratemeyer Adams died leaving behind a very large publishing company.

***

Several weeks after I discovered the treasures in my grandmother's trunk, I found myself browsing through a bookstore at the mall. I overheard two girls talking.

"Here they are, against the wall," one of the girls said excitedly.

"Wow, look how many there are!" the other girl exclaimed.

I followed them to the display rack where I saw at least a hundred paperback books displaying Nancy Drew involved in different adventures. Only, now, Nancy had a new compact car and longer, straight hair. Also, she was wearing jeans and a T-shirt and running shoes. Nancy Drew was a young college woman of the 1990s.

"Isn't she terrific?" I said to the girls.

"Yeah, I really like her a lot," one of the girls said as she took three books off the rack and started toward the cash register.

QUESTIONS AND ACTIVITIES

1.   Investigative reporters must report the news accurately. You, the reporter, have just been sent to the scene of a robbery to "get the story." What questions will you ask in order to get the most accurate information?

2.   Read one of the Nancy Drew books. What techniques did Harriet Stratemeyer Adams use to create suspense? What would you use to make a scene or story more exciting and suspenseful? Find a very short story you consider to be very dull. Rewrite it making it very exciting and interesting.

3.   Choose a TV detective (i.e. Jessica Fletcher). List all the things you like about this detective and all the things you don't like. Do you find this person believable or not? Why? Explain your answer.

4.   Go Fishing for Red Herrings! Many mystery writers put clues in their stories simply to confuse the detectives and readers. These clues are called "red herrings." Make up your own mystery. Put in all the necessary clues needed to solve the problem. Add 3-4 clues that don't have anything to do with the problem that could possibly confuse the detective. See if your classmates can find the red herrings.

6. Detectives rely on testimony of witnesses. Yet witnesses differ in describing the same scene. Look at the picture on page 83 for 12 seconds. Close the book and describe what you saw. Give as many details as possible.

7. Using the same picture, can you find several things that are illogical? Explain your discoveries.

8. Harriet Stratemeyer Adams accomplished many things in her lifetime. You, also, are very capable of accomplishing just as much, possibly more. Select the book you like best. Try writing your own book about those characters. Use the Stratemeyer formula. If you like what you have done, have your teacher go over it with you. Submit your book to a publisher. Who knows? You may begin a career in writing right now. Good luck!

A Street in Harriet's Town

CLASSROOM DISCUSSIONS AND ACTIVITIES

1. After reading at least one book in any of the series mentioned, make a list of how the characters are the same and how they are different. If you could change anything about any of these characters, what would it be? Explain your opinions. Back them up with facts. Comparing an old version of Nancy Drew with a new one, in what ways have women changed?

2. Produce an old-fashioned radio show. Be sure to include music and sound effects. Your local library may have audio tapes of the old radio show such as "The Shadow" and "Superman." Use these as models for your own show.

85--Better Than Our Best

Women "picking" silk in Paterson silk mill.
Circa 1900 Paterson, New Jersey

Courtesy of American Labor Museum
Botto House National Landmark
Haledon, New Jersey

HANNAH

SILVERMAN

"No time to go to school each day -

No time to spend your time at play"

"The golf links lie so near the mill
That almost everyday
The laboring children can look out
And see the men at play."

This poem was written over eighty years ago by Sarah Cleghorn when she saw men playing golf near a mill in the south in which young children were working. She wrote this in protest of child labor. People who were against young children working instead of going to school were known as reformers. For over one hundred years they worked to stop mill owners, farmers, or other employers all over America from hiring children to work long hours in a factory or field.

Many children were injured while working and many suffered from poor health because they had no time for rest or play. They had no chance to learn to read or write.

The National Child Labor Committee was started in 1904 to help change the law on child labor. School organizations, religious and women's groups, and labor unions worked together to prohibit child labor in every state of the United States. Some states had already passed their own child labor laws.

Finally, in 1938, Congress passed a law which said that children under 16 would not be allowed to work in most businesses. It also said that children under 18 could not work in manufacturing or in dangerous jobs. This did not end child labor, however; for the law did not protect agricultural work. Migrant workers traveling from farm to farm seeking work have children who cannot attend school regularly because the family must move on to wherever they are needed to help with the harvest.

The story of Hannah Silverman tells of a girl who had to leave school at an early age to work in a silk mill. Hannah, like so many children at that time, had to contribute to her family's income. It was the only way her family, like so many of the immigrants, could survive in the new world.

88--Women of Valor

Interior of a Throwing mill with young,
female operatives, circa 1900, Paterson, NJ

(Courtesy of American Labor Museum
Botto House, Haledon, N.J.)

HANNAH SILVERMAN

"No time to go to school each day-
No time to spend your time at play"

The story of Hannah Silverman tells of a brave girl who took a leading part in the great silk strike in Paterson, New Jersey, in 1913. Hannah was only seventeen years old when the strike began, and yet she became one of the leaders in a struggle which lasted almost five months. Her bravery showed what women could do in a labor dispute. As a fearless leader, she inspired others to stand firm for what they believed was right and just.

What brought about this strike? It began as a weaver protest against new looms which were more efficient and would eliminate the jobs of some weavers while increasing the work of others. By leaving many workers unemployed, these looms would bring hardship to their families. The workers were asking for higher wages and fewer working hours in talks they were having with the mill owners. When the mill owners refused to listen, the strike of the weavers was joined by the dye and ribbon weavers. Soon the strike spread to the three hundred mills which operated in Paterson at that time.

A labor union, the International Workers of the World (I.W.W.), came to help the workers in their strike. Union meetings were held at the Botto House in Haledon, New Jersey, because the Paterson police and the mayor of Paterson would not allow meetings to be held in the city.

When you read the following poem, you will discover a little more about Hannah Silverman and what happened to her and some of the strikers.

HANNAH SILVERMAN

Hannah Silverman, age seventeen
Joined the picket lines in 1913
In February's bitter cold
She marched with workers, young and old.

Who was this girl who was so brave?
Who never gave a thought to save
Her job for which she gave up all
To answer her fellow-workers' call?

We are not sure of her early life.
We know only of three months of strife,
In which she played a leading role
When Paterson's silk strike took its toll.

It is a mystery - what was she like?
What did she do before the strike?
Did she leave school at an early age
To add to her family's living wage?

Children left school in those days
At twelve or fourteen to learn the ways
Of becoming a helper at the mill,
And later, a weaver, if they learned the skill.

91--Better Than Our Best

Some tried to go to school at night,
And though they tried with all their might,
They found they could not keep awake.
A full day's work was enough to take.

We know that Hannah was seventeen
When she worked at a mill in 1913,
When Paterson's silk mills were its fame,
"Silk City of the World" was then its name.

Then one day, looms ceased to run;
A city silk-strike had begun,
New weaving looms had caused the trouble;
Cutting jobs in half, making mill-work double.

Three hundred mills went out on strike.
The workers marched, men, women, alike.
They walked before each red brick mill,
Believing it was a mission to fulfill.

When April came, Hannah had become
Captain of the picket line, and some,
Who could not stand the striker's pace,
Dropped out, but Hannah kept her place.

And when police, that April day
Carried her and her friends away,
She spent that night in city jail
But Hannah's spirit did not fail.

92--Women of Valor

Hannah with a will of iron
Hannah with a heart of a lion
Had walked to jail that soft spring day
Head held high - her price to pay.

Three times cell bars closed her in,
But she would not let injustice win
Hannah marched to protest a wrong.
She marched in time to a union song.

Into New York, the strikers brought
Their message, telling why they fought.
Like a beacon light, she led the way;
She shone above the rest that day.

By June the strikers knew they lost.
Hannah never counted what it cost.
Just a girl of seventeen -
Hero of an ugly scene.

Hannah had her shining hour.
She showed the world one woman's power.

WHAT BECAME OF HANNAH SILVERMAN

When the strike was over and the workers lost the fight for all they had worked for, Hannah went home. She has become "hero of the strike." No one knows for sure what she did in the nine years following the strike. Perhaps she no longer could find work as a weaver. It may be that because of her leadership in the strike, no mill owner would hire her.

She married at 26 and became a homemaker and mother of two children. Hannah worked with her husband, Harry Mandell, in a candy store they had bought in Paterson. She never told her children that she had been captain of a picket line or that she had been arrested and jailed three times for taking a major part in a labor dispute. They never knew that she had been a famous leader of the 1913 silk strike until many years after her death.

Hannah Silverman lived out her life quietly, perhaps often reliving "her shining hours" in her mind. She died in 1960, knowing that when others lost faith, she had kept hers, for the sake of all those who labor for a living.

THE SILK MILL WORKERS OF PATERSON

Who were the workers of these mills? They were mostly people of Europe who came to America to seek work and to escape from prejudice. In the 1840s, people came because not enough work was available in their own country. As the number of mills and the need for more workers grew, experienced weavers and spinners from Ireland, France, Italy, Switzerland, Poland, Russia, and Germany began arriving in great numbers. Later immigrants from Armenia, Syria, and Lebanon came to escape government persecution. They also brought with them textile experience. In the early 1900s, the growth of the dyeing industry brought workers from southern Italy and the Netherlands.

How did these people from so many lands manage to live in a country whose language they did not know when they first arrived? They joined friends, people from their native land, and, if possible, members of their family who had arrived before them grouped in neighborhoods according to their ethnic backgrounds. Many were able to build their own homes in villages not far from Paterson. Most of the neighborhoods were within walking distance to the mills. Those who lived farther away were able to take the trolley to work.

Churches, clubs, language newspapers, and social gatherings provided workers with the support they needed to help them adjust to their new homes in America. Sunday, the only day the mills were closed, was a day for picnics, music and dance, and other forms of recreation, such as card playing, gymnastics, and lawn ball (*bocce.*)

All members of a working class family helped to contribute to the family's income. Children ages 12 to 14 joined their relatives as workers in the mills. Since fathers could not support their families on what they earned, the whole family worked at the mill. The mother would bring food to her husband. She learned to do the weaving by watching and working alongside him. When the children were old enough, she brought them along to observe how the work was done and help do some of the work. These children dropped out of school early so their father could make more money by adding them as workers.

Women at home with infants helped with the family income by caring for boarders who rented rooms and by preparing food for these boarders. Young people who had no relatives or friends with whom they could live, rented rooms from families who needed more money to live. Read the advertisements below which were placed in a Paterson newspaper in 1890 (see Advertisement next page).

Typical Boarding Ads

97--Better Than Our Best

When the strike broke out, the children were not on the picket lines, but they attended the union meetings at the Botto House in Haledon where picnics were held while speeches about the strike were being made. Since most of their parents could not speak English, the children would translate or tell their parents what a worker from another country wanted to say.

As the months went by and their parents' money ran out, many of the children had little to eat. In fact, many who were suffering from malnutrition were fed by friends and relatives from other towns, and some were sent out of the city to live with these friends and relatives.

CLASSROOM DISCUSSION AND ACTIVITIES

1.   You have read a little about child labor in America. Why do you thing it took so long for Congress to pass child labor law for all the states?

2.   Migrant children still need help in getting an education. How would you go about helping them to have equal rights now? What could you do to help them if this problem still exists when you are older and have completed your education?

3.   You have read about the children of Paterson and how they faced their problems as children of immigrants. Discuss the problems of children of immigrants today. Do they face the same difficulties as children of the late 1890s or early 1900s?

4.   If you know of people in your family or friends of your family who came to America as children, talk to them about how they felt about their lives in America when they first arrived. Write a story about it to share with the class.

5.   Hannah Silverman.   In your opinion, was she brave or foolish to risk losing her job? What is your opinion of someone who risks all for their beliefs?

6. If you were Hannah Silverman, would you have taken part in that strike? Give your reasons.

7. On a world map locate the countries from which the silk mill workers came.

8. Imagine that you are one of these children. Choose a country from which your parents could have come. Tell how you feel and what you may have seen or heard about the strike. Or, tell about your life as a mill worker. Write it in diary form. Choose a date from April 1 to June 7, 1913.

Lena Frances Edwards

Courtesy of Schlesinger Library, Radcliffe College

LENA FRANCES EDWARDS

"Better Than Your Best"

The weather forecaster said, "Snow all day, ending at midnight tonight. The 'Siberian Express' has hit the East Coast." After dinner, in the Sanders house, two children were resting on the living room floor. The joy of the snow had left them too tired to argue about what program they would watch. They sat staring at the television set, as the weather report droned on.

Their parents, Mr. and Mrs. Sanders, were reading the evening newspaper. Anna Clinton, their grandmother, sat in her favorite chair writing her weekly column on local politics for the *Town News*.

"Who's choosing first for the program tonight?" asked Stacy. "Remember, we get one each."

Steve, her twin, lay on the carpet playing with Samantha, their Siamese cat.

"I'm too tired to choose. You pick one for me, Stacy."

"Boy, he must be tired," answered Mark, their older brother. Mark had stretched out on the couch. He was reading a book in the small sitting room next to the living room. His 14 year old body had grown long and thin. He was the "midnight oil-burner", the "student" of the family. Stacy and Steve, age twelve, still enjoyed a more carefree attitude toward school.

"I can't find any of our favorite shows," said Stacy, as she looked at the TV listings. "They're having specials tonight."

Steve looked over her shoulder at the *TV Guide*. "Rats," he said. "Now what'll we do?"

"You could read a good book," Mrs. Sanders said looking up from her paper. She smiled. "Books are still around, you know."

"I wanted to see an action show. You know. Courage! Daring! Adventure!"

"Here's just the book for you," said Mark. "*Profiles in Courage*." He held up the paperback.

"No," said Steve, "I want somebody to do the action for me."

Mrs. Clinton looked up from her writing. "I have an 'action' story I can tell you about someone who created the action and had courage! It's not the kind of action where tanks roll and planes dive. No, it's quiet, constructive action that needs courage and strength. This person received two medals for extraordinary service. So, do you want to hear the story?"

Stacy and Steve moved closer to her. Mark put down his book to listen. Mrs. Clinton leaned forward to catch their eyes.

"It doesn't start once upon a time, but it does begin in 1900 when a baby named Lena Frances Edwards was born. She was born into a middle class black family in Washington, D.C. Her father was a professor of dentistry at Howard University. Now, you're probably thinking, 'Oh, she must have had it easy in life.'"

"No," said Stacy. "I'm sure if you're telling us the story, she must have done something outstanding, Grandma."

Mrs. Clinton smiled. "Yes, honey, a fine home and money doesn't always mean you just sit back and feel you don't have to work hard. You have to make a better life for others, too."

Steve lay on the floor. Cupping his face with his hand, he asked, "But when does the action start, Grandma?"

"The action started when Lena was twelve - just your age. It was then she decided to become a doctor."

"Why?" asked Steve. "What made her do that?"

"Well, one day when her mother was ill, a friend who was a black female doctor came to take care of Mrs. Edwards. Lena saw and understood what she could do for people. As she grew up, she felt a strong sense of pride in her people and a duty to help others.

Mark put down his book and moved into the living room, closer to his grandmother. "How did she do it, Grandma?"

"She went to high school, studied hard," Mrs. Clinton glanced at Steve and Stacy, "and then was graduated from Howard University and Howard Medical School. She was married in 1925, the day after graduation, to her classmate, Keith Madison. He was a physician, too. They began their practices of medicine in Jersey City, New Jersey, that year.

"Two doctors in one family!" exclaimed Stacy.

"Lena Edwards' medical office was in the Lafayette section of Jersey City. She organized a group which opened a day nursery for children of working mothers, and then she visited the children to check them for disease and other problems. She spoke to teenagers at many churches in New Jersey. She also worked at Margaret Hague Hospital in Jersey City."

"Did she have any children?" asked Mrs. Sanders, who had put aside her newspaper to listen.

"Oh, yes, she had six children -- three girls and three boys: two doctors, a priest, a teacher, an engineer, and a social worker."

"My," said Mrs. Sanders, "and she accomplished all that work."

"There's more. After 29 years of being a doctor in private practice, she left Jersey City to teach at Howard University. There she became active in many organizations that helped the poor and needy. How's that for action, Steve?"

Steve said, "What else did she do? Is that the end of the story, Grandma?"

"No, there's more. When she was sixty she went to Texas to help the Mexican migrant workers and used her own money to help build a hospital for mothers and babies of the workers. Not only that, she supported the hospital from money she earned as a doctor for the ranchers' wives and non-Mexicans."

"What about the medals?" asked Steve.

"Well, the first one came from President Lyndon Johnson - the Presidential Medal of Freedom. This was for her contribution to society. The second one was a medal called the *Poverello*. She was proud of this. This honor is a religious one. It is given to people whose lives followed the ideals of St. Francis of Assisi. You see, Dr. Edwards gave away almost all of her personal wealth. This is what St. Francis did in his life. Dr. Edwards gave the money to establish a scholarship fund at Howard University Medical School."

"Wow," exclaimed Steve, "practically all her money."

Mrs. Clinton smiled. "More important, Steve, she gave of herself. Dr. Edwards returned to Jersey City when she was sixty-six and worked with anti-poverty programs while teaching at St. Peter's College."

"Did she ever have any fun?" asked Stacy.

"Yes, she loved sewing and gardening. These were her hobbies all her life."

"I guess after a while she just rested. She was pretty old." Steve nodded his head. He held Samantha, who had fallen asleep in his arms.

"No, she didn't rest. When she was seventy-two, she moved to Lakewood, New Jersey, near her daughter, Genevieve. Here she worked to improve health care for senior citizens and raised funds for students who could not afford to go to college without help."

Mr. Sanders shook his head. "What a remarkable life she had. Did she ever retire?"

"I think she spent the rest of her life helping others and accepting new challenges. She died in 1986." Mrs. Clinton got up from her chair.

"How do you know so much about Dr. Edwards, Grandma?" asked Steve.

"I read about her in a book on the history of women in America."

Stacy sighed. "I hope one day I'll be able to go to college. Maybe I'll try to get a Dr. Edwards scholarship, too."

"You must remember Grandma's story," said Mark. "It was hard work and courage that made Dr. Edwards the great woman she was."

"Yes," said Mrs. Clinton, "and remember her words 'Do not only your best, but even better than your best'."

QUESTIONS AND ACTIVITIES

1. Lena Edwards has been called a "Woman of Courage." Do you know a woman or man of courage? This person may be part of your own family or circle of friends. Perhaps it is someone you have heard about. Investigate this person's story and present it to your class in story form.

2. Lena Edwards knew at an early age that when she grew up she was going to become a doctor. Have you thought about what you would like to do with your life? Make a chart showing the kinds of things you would like to try. For example, you may want to explore being an astronaut, a mail carrier, a teacher, a scientist, a private detective, or a pilot. Be adventurous and have fun. Make your chart as colorful and as attractive as possible.

3. Lena Edwards did many worthwhile things with her life, yet she never sought public fame and glory. She could be called a quiet woman of worth. Talk with your parents and family members. Was there a woman in your family who did something that made her a woman of worth? For example, there could be a woman who worked extremely hard at great personal sacrifice in order for her family to have what they needed. Or, there could be a woman who created something new. Search through your own family for such a woman. Write a composition about her to be presented to your class.

BEATRICE HICKS

BEATRICE ALICE HICKS

"Bridges to Technology"

What do you want to be? How many times have you heard that question? It may be difficult to answer that question because you want to be so many things. Yet, some children know very early what they want to do with their lives. The story below is about one such child, Beatrice Alice Hicks.

On January 2, 1919, Beatrice Alice Hicks was born in Orange, New Jersey. She was the older daughter of William Lux Hickstein and Florence Benedict Hickstein. William Hickstein was a chemical engineer; Florence Hickstein was a homemaker who devoted herself to rearing their two daughters. Beatrice's younger sister, Margaret Lurene, was ten years younger than she and was mentally retarded. This caused the Hickstein family to experience both great sadness and joy. Eventually, Margaret Lurene was placed in a special school in Princeton, New Jersey.

When Beatrice was a young girl, she was fascinated with the many different kinds of bridges and buildings. She was curious about how they were built. When she discovered they were built by engineers, Beatrice decided to become one herself.

In school, the teachers realized that Beatrice had a gift for mathematics, physics, chemistry, and mechanical drawing -- some of the subjects engineers need in order to build great structures.

When Beatrice was twelve years old, she began to see her family suffer through the Great Depression. Mr. Hickstein lost his job at the Westinghouse Corporation. After some time, they had no money and had to give up their house. Having no place to live, they pitched a tent in the fields of Livingston, New Jersey. For a while, they ate only chopped beef and dandelion salad. Finally, Mr. Hickstein found a way to support his family. As a chemical engineer, he had designed a safety control that would automatically cut off hot water in steam heating systems. Even though money was very scarce during those terrible times, he was able to borrow money from a bank in order to market his design. At the site of an old apple cider mill in East Orange, Mr. Hickstein began his own company, the Newark Controls Company. Not only was he able to earn enough money for his family to move into a home, but this company would someday give Beatrice the opportunity to fulfill her dream of becoming an engineer. It was not easy, however. When Beatrice announced that she wanted to go to college and become an engineer, her teacher tried to talk her out of it. Her parents could not afford college for their older daughter because Margaret Lurene needed special care and attention that cost a great deal of money. Instead, they encouraged Beatrice to study stenography to become a secretary. Young Beatrice was determined, however, not to "just be taking notes," but to find a way to pay for her studies.

In 1935, Beatrice graduated from Orange High School. In order to study engineering at the Newark College of Engineering (now the New Jersey Institute of Technology), she worked as a sales clerk in a department store during the day and as a telephone switchboard operator at night. Beatrice Hicks became one of the only two women out of 900 students studying engineering at the college. It was during this period that she changed her name from Hickstein to Hicks.

In 1939, Beatrice Hicks graduated from college and began to work at Western Electric in Kearny where Bell Telephone, now New Jersey Bell, did most of its manufacturing. In spite of her engineering degree, however, the firm refused to give her the title of "engineer" because Beatrice was a woman. Instead, she was referred to as a "technician." Many co-workers were very suspicious of her. It seemed as if they did not think her sufficiently capable or trustworthy to perform such a job. Beatrice herself said, "At first, some of the men acted as if I alone would sabotage the entire World War II effort then in progress."

Beatrice Hicks was able to gain the respect and trust of her co-workers by proving herself through her work. She designed and developed crystal oscillators to control radio frequencies in aircraft communications equipment. This was her first major accomplishment.

Even though Beatrice Hicks was working as an engineer, she continued to go to college. In this way, she could keep up with all the new engineering developments as they came along. Her work was so good that she was promoted and her salary was increased. Finally, she received the title of engineer. Despite these accomplishments, Beatrice Hicks left the company in 1945. She said, "I was being well paid and was getting ahead, but it was fundamentally a man's world there."

When her father died, Beatrice Hicks stepped into his shoes and became the director of engineering at Newark Controls. She was in charge of a 22 man team who designed, developed, and made electro-mechanical heat controls. It was during this period that she married Rodney D. Chip on August 12, 1948.

Between the years of 1951 and 1955, Beatrice Hicks co-founded and was president of the Society of Women Engineers. This was an organization that would help girls and women find careers in engineering if they wanted. She said, "Women think that an engineer is a man in hip boots building a dam. They don't realize that 95% of the work is done in a nice air-conditioned office."

In 1955, Beatrice Hicks took full charge of Newark Controls. She designed, developed, and produced environmental sensors and controls for ground, aircraft, and aerospace use. She invented many other controls that helped many different industries.

Beatrice Hicks was always interested in making people understand what engineering was all about. She gave many talks to children's groups. She gave a very simple explanation:

"An engineer has to be able to see and think in three-dimensions, structural visualization. Dress designers have this ability; so does anyone who ever made a slipcover. Mathematics? That's just measuring. A slipcover marker has to be a good measurer."

Beatrice Hicks accomplished many things in her life. Not only did she invent many items that added to our technology today, but she opened the door for many young girls and women to become engineers. In 1963, the Society for Women Engineers gave her an award for all her accomplishments. She was honored by Rensselaer Polytechnic Institute as the first woman to be awarded an honorary degree.

On October 21, 1979, at age 60, Beatrice Hicks died of a heart attack while visiting her sister. She is buried in Arlington National Cemetery next to her husband.

INVENTIONS AND ACCOMPLISHMENTS

1. Gas density switch - necessary to space travel.

2. Air to ground communication and ignition switches - used for the second stage of Saturn V, used in Apollo and Surveyor rockets.

3. Trouble Analyzer - signals a monitor or ground control operator that enclosed electronic parts are in danger of disintegrating by burning up.

4. A new way to think about and apply gas laws - gas density in a sealed area. A pilot would have a switch to signal that there was a leak or other problem.

5. Sensors for different functions:

    a. Sound an alarm if the stress on the frame of a plane, missile, or rocket is affected by the speed of the craft.

    b. Monitor the level of fuel in jets, rockets, and missiles.

    c. Warn about switches that do not function properly.

    d. Monitor the rate of flow of fuels and liquids.

    e. Indicate dangerous densities of gas or liquid.

QUESTIONS AND ACTIVITIES

Make a bridge about your life. Try to give as much information about yourself as you can: family background, what obstacles you have come across, what you have accomplished so far, what you would like to accomplish, and tell about any dreams you have for the future. Make your bridge in any way that you feel really represents you by drawing, building, sewing, carving, etc.. Be as creative as you can be.

CLASSROOM DISCUSSIONS AND ACTIVITIES

1. Beatrice Hicks had many obstacles to overcome as she grew up. She used these obstacles to her advantage in order to reach her goal. Have a class discussion about how you can turn a negative obstacle into a positive support in your own life.

2. Divide the class into 4 groups. Each group should list the many different kinds of bridges. Each group will decide which are the most unusual kinds of bridges and draw pictures of those bridges for a display in the classroom.

3. Beatrice Hicks said mathematics is "only measuring." See if you can invent your own system of measurement. Try to make it as simple and as clear as you can. Pretend you are inventing this system for people who know nothing about measuring.

COMPARISON CHART

Molly Pitcher, Cornelia Hancock, and Elizabeth White lived in different time periods of our history. Compare their lives by filling in the chart. Use separate sheet of paper for your work.

	Molly Pitcher	Cornelia Hancock	Elizabeth White
Place of birth			
Time in history woman lived			
Education			
Occupation			
What made each woman important in history			

CHECK YOUR KNOWLEDGE.....

Revolutionary   Monmouth
Mary Ludwig Hays McCauley   thirsty
carrying   cannon
hero

Molly Pitcher's real name was _____

_____ _____.

She was known for her bravery at the Battle
of _____ where she loaded and fired
a _____. This battle was fought during
the_____ War. Molly was also
known for_____ water to tired and
_____soldiers. Molly Pitcher was
called a _____.

119--Better Than Our Best

South Carolina   wounded   school   country
writing   nurse   ten   food
volunteered   Gettysburg   freed

Cornelia Hancock was a _____ in the
army. She helped serve at _____ in
Pennsylvania. There she tended to _____
soldiers. She helped by _____ letters home
to family and friends. She also helped serve them
_____. She _____ her time.
Her dream was to serve her _____.
Later, Cornelia Hancock started a _____
for _____ slave children. Her school was
in _____ _____. She
stayed on as a teacher for _____ years.

young   accident   school
uncle   Massachusetts   high school
manage   Normal School   classrooms
Blind   first chief   Braille

Lydia Hayes was blinded in an _____. She
was _____ when this happened. Her parents sent
her to live with an _____ and to be educated in a
_____ for the blind. This school was in
_____. She stayed on through
_____ _____. She then studied at
Boston Kindergarten _____ _____
where she was given a job to _____
a private nursery school for sighted children.
In 1909, she was selected to organize the
New Jersey Commission for the _____. After one
year, Governor Woodrow Wilson appointed her the
_____ _____ executive officer of the commission.
A house in Newark was used for social rooms,
_____, workshops and offices. After a while,
with the work done by Lydia Hayes and others, New
Jersey allowed public schools to conduct classes in
_____.

121--Better Than Our Best

scientist   cranberry
bogs   blueberry
Whitesbog   Frederick Coville
interested   cultivated
packing   market

Elizabeth White was born on her father's _____
farm in New Lisbon, New Jersey. She was a self-
taught _____. Her family's farm was named
_____. She helped on the farm working in the
_____. Later she became more _____ in the
farm and worked in the _____ and shipping
department. She loved being on the farm. In 1911,
White wrote to _____ _____ and invited
him to continue his research on cultivating the
_____ at the farm. Together they developed
the _____ blueberry and brought it to
_____.

built	engineer	Hicks
Building	invented	women
George	dream	engineer
Bridge	engineer	Society of Women

Beatrice _____ always dreamed of becoming an
_____. She was always fascinated with the
_____ Washington _____ and the Empire State
_____. She was curious about how they were
_____.   Her father was a chemical _____
who formed the Newark Controls Company. This
company enabled Hicks to fulfill her _____ of
being an engineer. At first she worked for Western
Electric where she designed communication equipment.
Later she took over Newark Controls Company when
her father died. She _____ many controls that
helped many different industries. Hicks co-founded
and was president of the _____ ____ _____
Engineers. She opened the doors for many
young _____ to be engineers.

Using the words below, write a paragraph on Hannah Silverman.

silk strike	leader
weaver	looms
hardship	family
mill owner	ribbon weaver
labor union	police
brave	march

GLOSSARY

Look up definitions of each glossary entry. Find out how many different ways the word can be used. For example, can it be used both as a noun and/or as a verb, such as:

compress, noun - com´press - a folded cloth or pad applied to an injury.

compress, verb - com press´ - to press together, to reduce in size or volume.

Find as many synonyms as you can for each entry. Also list antonyms and if there are any, homonyms. Use each word in a sentence.

Chapter - Molly Pitcher - Mary Ludwig Hays McCauley
cannon
colonist
commemorative
distinguished
domestic
enlisted
immigrant
petticoat

Chapter - Cornelia Hancock
convalescing
fetch
fictitious
medal
pews
portray
revered
social work

Chapter - Lydia Young Hayes
route
memory
opportunity
volunteered
tutoring
appoint
Braille

Chapter - Elizabeth Coleman White
self-taught
scientist
graduate
migrant workers
pioneer
retraction
controversy
market
propagation
cellophane
horticulture
research

Chapter - Alice Paul
vote
amendment
injustice
community
dedicated
authority
elected
discriminate

campaign
reform
rights
ratify

Chapter - Harriet Stratemeyer Adams
adventure
amaze
authentic
detect
disband
discover
edit
entertain
fascinate
formula
humor
imagine
inherit
intrigue
series
syndicate

Chapter - Hannah Silverman
labor
contribute
protest
income
homemaker
strike
prohibit
picket

union
industry

Chapter - Lena Frances Edwards
forecaster
politics
courage
pride
physician
organizations
scholarship
challenges

Chapter - Beatrice Alice Hicks
aerospace
flight
suffer
manufacture
trustworthy
technician
ability
visualize
experience
oscillate
environment
accomplishment
milestone

Rebus

The puzzle below is called a *Rebus*. It has pictures of objects and signs. Sound out their names to find the missing words or phrases.

Answer:

Be the best you can be and explore every potential.